NOTES
from Your
FAIRY
GODMOTHER

Ideas, Inspiration and Joy

DIANE BUCCOLA

Copyright © 2017 Diane Buccola

All rights reserved.

ISBN: 0998670901
ISBN-13: 978-0-9986709-4

DEDICATION

To those wonderful souls who share their creativity with the world through their words, music, art and kindness. Thank you for the light and sparkle that you bring to the world.
And a special thanks to my friends at Happy Esthetician.

CONTENTS

	Foreword	i
1	Introduction	1
2	The Path	3
3	The Culprit	5
4	The Moments	7
5	The Reality	11
6	The Clutter	13
7	The Solution	15
8	The Perspective	17
9	The Joy	19
10	The Beauty	21
11	The Magic	23
12	The Inspiration	29

You had the Power all along, my dear.

~ Glinda, the Good Witch

FOREWORD

Change your perspective, change your life.

Life is a collection of moments and in each moment, we have choices to make. Those choices, individually and collectively, define the trajectory of our lives. Why then aren't we running at full speed toward our dreams?

Although there are wonderful things raining down all around us, we can't always see them because of the wall that has been built from our constant exposure to negative and unrealistic info. This wall keeps us apart from our intuition, inspiration and our most creative ideas. We had easy access to all these things when we were children but as we've grown up, so has the wall.

The good news is that these important tools of life are still there, and they still belong to us. Oh, we can manage to live without them, of course, but it will be a bumpier ride than it needs to be. Once you clear the clutter, clarity of thought will step in to take its place. Your perspective will no longer be under the influence of television commercials, magazine ads, social media chatter, reality shows and TV news.

There is no long and difficult process required to reclaim your lost self. There are no rules, nothing you must purchase, no groups you must join. It's actually pretty simple, and it's free.

If you clear a little space, well-being will seep in through the cracks...*and therein lies the joy.*

This book includes over 200 inspirational, motivational and humorous reflections that I have collected over the years. While there is much wisdom to be gleaned from historical figures such as Albert Einstein, Martin Luther King, Jr. and F. Scott Fitzgerald, there are also wonderful gems to be found in the poets, authors, and posters of today.

I have done my best to research and credit authors of the quotes, however, many have been repurposed so many times that the original content was almost unrecognizable. When I was successful at tracking down the original version and its author, I included it.

I hope you will enjoy this little book as much as I have enjoyed creating it for you. .

To the life of your dreams,
Diane

1. INTRODUCTION

I have been a licensed Esthetician in California since 1999, as well as nationally certified since 2008. During my career, I have been a spa owner, speaker, author, trainer, mentor, event planner, producer, and role model. Most Estheticians are women and most of our clients are women, so over the years I have been exposed to many thousands of women via various components of my career.

This exposure has given me the opportunity to peek inside the psyches of women. I know their fears, I know their dreams, and I've seen their obstacles. For example, I cannot count the number of women I have heard lament over their lost youth. They long for their skin/brows/butt of 10 years ago, and my response is always the same: 10 years from now, it's *today's* butt/brows/skin you will be longing for. So don't miss it! Unfortunately, we often fail to appreciate things until we've lost them.

> Dear Fairy Godmother:
> Think you could bippity-boppity-boo me back to 21 years old and that awesome body I thought was so fat?
> Thanks.

The title "Notes from Your Fairy Godmother" was inspired by the quote, *"What if your fairy godmother is the wisest, smartest version of yourself, whispering from the future?"* This book is based upon the idea of learning in layers, such as: A-ha moment, waking up, letting go, distraction, new desires, and movement toward something new. For example:

- Identify the external forces that are currently impacting your everyday life in a negative way. *"If you want to clean the house, you've got to look at the dirt." (Louise Hay)*

- Once the external forces have been identified, you can implement solutions and take control of the abundance of incoming information which will then result in a shift away from negative external forces.
- And lastly, finding inspiration which will keep you on your path to motivation and joy. Repetitive reading has proven to enhance absorption of an idea, therefore if a student is not provided with tools to use on a regular basis to keep the momentum going and the dream alive, the enlightenment can fade very quickly. This book is one of those tools.

You may not even realize that you have inadvertently been practicing anxiety and stress. To turn that around, you've got to practice Happy instead.

You may also not realize that you have an internal navigation system, also sometimes known as gut feeling, intuition, or inspiration. It's always there, but you may not be taking advantage of this powerful tool. To take it for a test run, simply think of something that brings you joy or makes you laugh. Note how that feels. Then compare that to how you feel when you think of something sad or stressful. The difference is palpable, and you can use this guidance to identify which things feel best to you as you sort through them.

The beauty of this life is that everyone gets to blaze their own trail, and go their own way. There are many paths to happiness, and this book just happens to offer one of them. As you begin to apply the principles of this book, the first thing you might feel is relief. Like you can breathe, and maybe even relax a bit. Then perhaps moments of joy will begin to appear. These might feel familiar; in other words, you will recognize these moments as something you once had but haven't experienced in a long while.

And then when you go back to your usual sources of stress, you will be much more in tune with how those stressors make you feel. This awareness will help you take control of your life, and you'll begin to appreciate and rely on your internal guidance. That's what empowerment feels like!

2. THE PATH

**Don't wait for someone to bring you flowers.
Plant your own garden and decorate your own soul.**

My position in the beauty industry for over two decades has given me an unobstructed view of the power that society has over women. In my opinion, this is an ongoing targeted attack which has resulted in too many of today's women making choices based upon self-loathing rather than self-care. For these women, "personal transformation" means physical beauty. They may try a new lover, a new body, a new face…but these too will fade, and the stress of life will continue.

Most women are simply looking for reasons to be satisfied with themselves in the present, however, they are looking for self-love in all the wrong places. Regrettably, it is often not until a state of crisis occurs such as illness, substance abuse, trauma, or depression that a woman is finally compelled to seek out answers, solutions, and tools to survive. I would like to reach that woman before crisis compels her to seek new life skills.

The tools I am teaching in this book have always been part of my perspective, and all aspects of my career and my life are peppered with it. In fact, people often quote *me* back to *me*, which is the highest compliment of all. Because of that, I feel the time has come that I must get the information contained in this book into the hands of as many women as possible. I truly believe these tools can transform the lives of women everywhere, just as they have transformed mine.

To be clear, I am not suggesting that my way is necessarily the only way. I am simply suggesting that women wake up to their own power. "Notes from Your Fairy Godmother" is designed to help women identify the external forces that are currently guiding their lives, so they can begin to dust off their dreams and reclaim their joy. I am suggesting to women that they turn down the external volume and listen to their own inner voice which will allow them to tap into their internal guidance system. If heeded, it will not lead them astray.

3. THE CULPRIT

"You look happy," said anxiety. "Let me fix that."

On the surface, many women appear to have everything: the happy marriage, great kids, successful career. But below the surface, she is holding her life together by a single safety pin. (I know this woman because periodically I am this woman.) Today's women have become extreme multitaskers as they juggle career and/or family, and rarely does self-care make it to the top of their priority list.

Throughout my decades in the esthetics business, I have seen the industry's focus go from self-care to paranoia regarding the inevitable aging process. It has been difficult to watch this phenomenon as it continues to dramatically diminish the self-worth of many women.

Throughout my over 2 decades in the esthetics business, I have witnessed every iteration of M.D. create a "spa" and -- without going into too many specific, scientific and gory details -- let me just say that many women are now pursuing "beauty" based solely upon society's definition. Every day, women are having layers of skin removed to dangerous levels via aggressive peels, sharp blades or needles, to the point that blood is drawn.

Media

Many women will turn to light-weight movies as a break from reality. It is an escape. We know there will be a handsome man, a snowball fight, and a dog. It's predictable, it's comfy, and it doesn't take a lot of brain power to process. So we curl up with our cup of tea or glass of wine in eager anticipation of a few feel-good hours. And then come the commercials.

I noticed a long time ago the abundance of TV commercials

designed to create worry, fear, and insecurity in the female audience. For purposes of research for this book, I recorded and watched a movie that premiered on Hallmark channel during Christmas season. You might expect to see a lot of Christmas-related ads, but that was not the case.

There were 60 commercials, half of which fell into the fear/worry, beauty/aging categories. Even if I listed for you the name and function of these products or services, it wouldn't adequately translate for you the theme and tone of the verbiage and images used to make women feel specific emotions associated with these products, such as fear and anxiety. I'm sure you can imagine how much damage can be done in 30 seconds with the use of carefully crafted video and dialogue.

I am not suggesting women stop watching television; nor am I suggesting these ads are not useful in some way. And I am definitely not picking on the Hallmark channel because the same is true with all channels and all TV shows that appeal to a female audience. I am only suggesting by this example that women watch Hallmark movies to feel good, to detach from whatever stressors they may have in their day or in their life, yet 50% of the advertisements pull women right back to thoughts of ill health, imperfections, beauty flaws, and other things to be afraid of.

4. THE MOMENTS

Chin up Princess...or the tiara slips.

My many years in the beauty business is the basis for my current belief that there is a void in women's lives, and somebody needs to be the life raft to save these women. I realize this is a big task, but I am willing to chip away at it. I believe my credentials, expertise and reputation in the spa/beauty industry are the reasons women will trust me. However, my grasp of the female psyche began long before my esthetics career.

Many experiences in my life have brought me to my passion for helping women. I would like to tell you about a couple of my most noteworthy a-ha moments so that you will understand that my passion for helping women navigate life with joy runs deep and far.

The Model

My family owned upscale women's clothing stores in Central California for 25 years. I started helping out when I was 12, making bows and wrapping gifts during Christmas season. As I got older, I moved up through the ranks, unpacking and steaming newly-arrived shipments of clothing, and eventually I became a salesperson and occasional model.

There was a very well-respected women's business organization that hosted an annual fashion show for which my family's stores provided the clothing, and another family member's salon provided hair and makeup. I modeled in the annual fashion show for years, even after I had left the family business. My last modeling gig involved a tandem walk with the newly-elected

Miss California. It was watching the video of that walk that convinced me I was never going to be a supermodel. (Suffice it to say, my self-esteem took a hit that day!)

Dear younger me:
You will get better with age.

Leading up to the annual fashion show, a call was put out to women in the area inviting them to apply for a makeover which would be revealed on stage several weeks later during the fashion show. As I recall, 5 or 6 women were chosen based upon applications they sent in. This six-week process involved nutritional counseling, an exercise program, and styling of hair, makeup and clothing. For many years, my cousin and I also worked a couple of nights a week teaching aerobics at a local health club, so we were put in charge of the 6-week exercise program for our makeover candidates.

The letters we received from women applying for the makeover came from all ages; young mothers all the way to grandmothers. And they all shared one thing: they did not feel good about themselves anymore. Even though at the time, I was in my early 20s, unmarried with no children, I was moved by these letters. And that experience was the source of my first a-ha moment on the topic of women's psyches.

Every year, the highlight of the fashion show was seeing these women step on the stage and walk down the runway to debut their new look. It was so amazing! It wasn't what they were wearing or how their hair or makeup looked, it wasn't even the applause from the audience that brought all of us to tears. It was the smile on these women's faces, the way they carried themselves on the runway. (I still get chills when I think about it!) Their joy was palpable, and I loved every moment of it. I'm quite sure this is what eventually led me to a career in the beauty business.

The Mom

Another of my earliest a-ha moments came soon after the birth of my son. He arrived earlier than expected and he required feeding every two hours which meant I had to find ways to keep myself awake during mealtimes. The best middle-of-the-night option was TV, however back then, there really were only two acceptable choices. One was talk show reruns, and the other was Nick at Nite, which at the time I wasn't all that familiar with.

I started with the talk shows because I assumed those would engage my mind and thereby hold my attention better and longer than kid's shows would. But I soon realized that by watching these late night talk shows, I was becoming more and more sad and depressed. Eventually I figured out this was due to the smarmy "reality TV" content, but at the time I blamed it on a cumulative lack of sleep. I tired of the talk show content relatively quickly and I switched to option 2, the Nick at Nite shows which to my surprise, turned out to be old sitcoms. Almost instantly upon changing channels, I felt much better, even though the feeding schedule had not changed, nor had my sleep deprivation. This was an enormous lesson that changed the trajectory of my life: *What you ingest into your mind has an impact on your psyche.*

5. THE REALITY

*Just when the caterpillar thought the world was over,
she became a butterfly.*

    The moment when a woman ceases to feel beautiful can happen at any time in her life; in fact, statistics show it is happening to very young girls who are desperately trying to live up to the artificial standards of reality stars and social media influencers.

    One might assume that millennial supermodels are the only ones who feel beautiful all the time, but if you have ever heard or seen an interview with those who are willing to speak publicly (and honestly) about their experience, oftentimes the struggle to be skinny and beautiful makes them very unhappy. That said, I fear that millennials are being held captive by technology, so it may take a while for them to discover that true happiness and beauty will not come from makeup, likes and selfies.

    Although my background is in the beauty industry, I am not out to extinguish the business of beauty. I am simply trying to wake women up to the fact that they are drowning in overexposure to female-targeted marketing designed to make us worry; for example, to be fearful of crimes, illnesses and other common issues of aging. The attack is never-ending, and it comes from many directions. And the worst part? We unknowingly pass these fears along to our daughters, thereby implanting the "you-are-not-enough" mentality, which makes them targets for bullying.

*Nothing has a stronger influence on a child
than the unlived life of a parent.
~ Carl Jung*

6. THE CLUTTER

**My desire to be well-informed is currently at odds
with my desire to remain sane.**

Whether you look at it from a scientific or spiritual perspective, evidence clearly supports the fact that there is a mind-body connection. Therefore, exposure to constant negativity and fear not only gets in the way of our joy, but it adds to our stress and anxiety levels which can ultimately impact our health.

It's interesting to note the disparity between the careful thought people give when deciding what they will ingest into their body via food sources, as compared to the lack of thought given to what they will allow into their mind. For example, many believe that a diet high in fat, sugar or processed foods will negatively impact their health, but the same consideration is rarely given to the elements of the content allowed into their mind.

To put this into perspective, consider the fact that few of us would ever walk into a restaurant and say to the server, "I don't need a menu. Just bring me whatever you want me to eat and I'll eat it." Yet most of us absorb whatever information is presented to us from various external sources without considering the long-term effect on our health and our life.

Negative aspects are all around us and always will be. We are reminded of this every day via television commercials offering us products and services to protect us against crimes which in all probability we will never encounter, and medical conditions we didn't know we had, probably don't, and likely never will.

The power of suggestion is potent, and very lucrative for vendors.

But for us, it causes a shift in perspective -- away from the lightness and fun in life. The good news is that once we become aware of the sources of anxiety consistently being thrown at us, we can choose to do something about it.

7. THE SOLUTION

**The best vacation from stress
is a mind filled with Happy Thoughts.**

Whatever relaxes your mind, also relaxes your body. It doesn't matter what you have been through in the past. If you learned something, then it wasn't a waste of time. And sometimes, the best way to determine what you do want is to clarify what you don't want. So leave all of that in the past and don't look back, because you're not going that way. Simply decide what you want right now and set off to make it happen.

What makes you happy? What makes your heart skip a beat? You can't rely on other people for your happiness, because ultimately you have no control over their behavior. So let's leave that out and stick to things you have around you that perhaps you occasionally catch a glimpse of, or think about briefly, but have historically dismissed without much contemplation. You might be surprised at the happy surprises and joyful discoveries that are right in front of you.

When you begin to change your focus and actively add uplifting and fun things into your life, your mind may seem to be playing a tennis match for a while. Back and forth, back and forth your thoughts will go. Good v. bad, happy v. stressed, positive v. negative. The great news about this process is that it will highlight very clearly for you the anxiety-ridden thoughts that have been trespassing in your mind for longer than you can remember.

Of course, we cannot block out all of the unpleasant things that surround us, nor should we try. But our perspective of the world impacts our life in a powerful way. So taking control of what and how we ingest information is essential for a balanced and happy life.

If you believe you could use a little more joy in your life, experiment with the ideas in this book for a day, a week, or more. The results will be swift and empowering. I know that the thought of unplugging from familiar things can be a bit daunting at first, but just remind yourself that anything you may have missed will not have vanished. You will simply have turned your attention away from it briefly, and everything can be easily retrieved..

Imagination is the only weapon against reality. And while you may not be able to change the world, you can certainly shift your perspective and change *your* world. And that's when life gets really fun.

8. THE PERSPECTIVE

Perspective is everything.

These days, exposure to negative information seems to dominate the airwaves and internet, with mainstream news sources being a common culprit. Here is an example of two perspectives regarding a popular topic: auto accidents. Both are factual, but each will shift your perspective in a different direction:

Millions of people drive down our freeways every day. There are many variables involved in this journey such as the driver's skill level, experience, health, age, level of stress, eyesight, hearing, attitude, sense of direction, and language barriers. There are also variables related to the vehicles they are driving such as age, brand, maintenance history, condition of the tires and other moving parts. And there are general distractions related to road conditions, construction, traffic, and weather.

Despite all these variables, those millions of cars and their millions of drivers arrive safely at millions of destinations every day without incident. Isn't that amazing when you really think about it?

Yet the stories that consistently make headlines are the gory fatal accidents -- complete with graphic photos and video -- which may occur in a city we've never heard of; in a state we've never visited.

I am not suggesting that gory accidents and murders aren't interesting to some, but our perspective of the world not only has a profound impact on our own daily life, but it extends to everyone around us.

The ultimate goal is simply to be mostly happy as we go through the ups and downs of life. This does not mean that you should abandon your beliefs or not stand up for or against causes that are important to you. This is only to suggest that you unplug once in a while in order to recharge your batteries and take care of yourself.

9. THE JOY

**Sometimes you need to talk to a 3-year-old
so you can understand life again.**

      Joy is an internal process for us all. Children are born knowing that they are enough, and it's not until lack and fear is put upon them by their environment that they attach to an identity and begin responding to conditions.
      This is a problem because the rest of the world is not here to appease us. Humans are going to do what they are going to do based upon their own backgrounds, beliefs, wishes, dreams, and life experience. So if you expect to control conditions or demand that others comply with your view of the world, you're going to be out of luck and not very happy.
      Here's an analogy that will help clarify the futility of relying on external conditions in order to be balanced and happy:

> Imagine you are standing in a swimming pool and you have carefully arranged several ping pong balls in a perfect circle around you. Each ping pong ball represents something important in your life such as a child, spouse, job, self-image, the state of your country or the world.
>
> Even as you play your part perfectly in this scenario and stand motionless in the pool, those ping pong balls are going to go their own way. They will drift in different directions and at various speeds, due to conditions that have nothing to do with you and which are completely out of your control. It would be a stressful and ultimately futile effort to try to control those ping pong balls,

and it would be a very unsatisfying experience.

The moral of this story is that if we need those ping pong balls to align with our wishes, needs, or beliefs in order for us to be happy, we are in trouble. Our goal should be to find ways to keep ourselves in balance without relying on anyone else, because only then can we stay our own course no matter what the conditions may be. So forget about those uncooperative ping pong balls and instead go for a wonderful swim or float in that pool!

Everyone knows what it feels like to be around a joyful person. They leave the room a little brighter than when they entered it. A joyful person is a gift…to themselves, to their family, to their friends, and to the world.

10. THE BEAUTY

I identify more with who I feel myself to be than what I look like. Either way, am I obliged to entertain you with my appearance?

~ Carrie Fisher

Because I have been in the beauty industry since 1999, I can tell you that making women feel they are "not enough" has become big business over the years.

Women are regularly exposed to ad campaigns suggesting that we should lose weight, exercise more, eat this, don't eat that. There are age-shaming ads implying that we need to fix something. We are encouraged to lift, tuck, flatten, lose, add, remove, install, inject, cut, dye, lengthen, shorten, ingest a supplement, sign up for a program, or model ourselves after celebrities.

As a result of this marketing strategy, self-image takes up a lot of space in the minds of many women. In fact, it clutters our minds to the point that we are unable to appreciate our own beauty as we continue to evolve throughout our lives. We are typically our own worst critic; however, our criticisms are not based upon who we really are, but rather who we think we should be according to input from external sources.

What woman hasn't at one time or another said to herself (or to others), "I hate my _____" (arms, legs... *fill in the blank*)?

We weren't born this way, but we have unintentionally picked up this burden and we carry it with us every day of our lives. If we could eliminate the self-critical thinking, can you imagine all the extra space we'd have in our brains to think about other, more pleasant things? If only we could enlighten girls about this at a younger age, what a wonderful life experience they would have!

By no means do I mean to imply that women should avoid all anti-aging efforts, because I really don't feel that way. Certainly, if something makes you feel good, do it. But the methods offered for improvement are becoming further invasive and frighteningly extreme.

Many great ideas come from fashion and beauty resources, of course, but we've got to find a way to keep everything in perspective and not abandon our spirit while chasing physical perfection.

Agelessness v. Beauty

Agelessness is not an actual destination; it is a marketing concept directed at women. So no matter how hard we try or how much money we spend, we'll never get there because the finish line is always moving.

Beauty, on the other hand, means many things, few of which are based on something as temporary as looks. There is beauty in love, kindness, friendship, children, nature, the heart, the soul, and memories of a life well-lived.

Yet we continue to compare ourselves with a very narrow view of beauty as dictated by fashion and beauty "experts," even though we are aware of the manipulation by airbrushing and photoshopping, as well as fake hair, extreme diets, and the various teams of people who prepare models and celebrities before their images are presented to us.

You know what they say: Sometimes the grass looks greener on the other side…because it's fake.

Be your own kind of beautiful.

11. THE MAGIC

*Even though she was scared, she pulled herself together
and headed in the direction of her dreams.*

FINDING YOUR JOY

Below are some ideas to get you started with the principles outlined in this book. These suggestions are simply intended to stimulate your own imagination, because this only works if you are doing things *your* way by tapping into things that make *you* happy.

Most of these ideas cost nothing, other than a little time – which you will have in abundance due to the absence of things from which you have temporarily unplugged. If possible, begin early in your day before the usual stressors have had a chance to fall upon you. If that is not possible, at least spend time throughout your day enjoying the thought of the fun things you intend to do later.

Do this as often as works for you, such as one day per week, one entire week, or longer -- anything you can do to give yourself some relief and allow creativity, clarity and joy to come flowing in.

THINGS TO EXTRACT/REMOVE/AVOID

Commercials. Hit the mute button or fast-forward through all of them. Even if you are not actively listening to the ads, if the sound is on, that info is getting into your brain. By actively hitting the mute button, you will become aware of how often this stuff is coming at you.

Articles. Avoid those "you're-not-good-enough-as-you-are-and-here's-how-you-can-be-better (younger-prettier-thinner, etc.)" articles. It gives a false sense of reality based upon a very narrow view of beauty and an unrealistic goal of perfection.

Friends. This applies to personal friends, co-workers, and social media connections. Just for a while, spend the majority of your time with those who make you happiest, those who make you laugh and those who help you feel great about yourself. (And be very grateful for them!) There is no need to announce to anyone that you are going to pull your attention away from anyone, just do it quietly. Their feedback would likely be more of a hindrance than helpful.

News. Next time you watch TV News, carefully assess the slant of the teases and lead stories. See if you notice a lean toward fear-inducing stories, or those that are gratuitously gory or sad. If you see a headline or hear about a development you are interested in knowing more about, do your own fact search online. Stick to facts, not opinions. Look for interviews that come from those who were actually involved as opposed to editorials and opinions.

Social Media. The best option is to ignore your personal pages completely if you can do it. But if the thought of that is too painful, then at least don't read the comments from people you don't know; especially related to news articles, politics and current events. People want to be relevant, and social media provides a captive audience which allows them to post things they would never have the guts to say in person. Don't allow yourself to be part of their audience; don't give the haters and the bullies any power.

- Don't be afraid to block, delete, unfriend or unfollow negative people. Try it for a while and if you change your mind, you can "follow" or "friend" them again.

THINGS TO DO/ADD/ENJOY

Meditation. I am using this term loosely. I am not specifically referring to the traditional ritual which involves a certain period of time and a specific goal. I mean just get comfortable and for 5-10 minutes, focus your mind on something easy and pleasant. Then close your eyes and breathe normally. To help distract and calm your mind, here are a few suggestions:

- Calming music or nature sounds from your own playlist or from YouTube. Just be sure the source doesn't have commercials or anything that will interrupt the process.
- Sit outside and contemplate the clouds, feel the breeze or the warm sun on your body.
- Focus on any repetitive white noise, such as your clothes dryer, air conditioner, or anything that won't start and stop.
- This sort of meditation works best if you do it early in the day before your everyday life invades your mind and blocks your access to that neutral space.
- Just before going to sleep is another important time to clear your mind because whatever you are thinking about as you drift off to sleep will be waiting for you when you wake up. So choose carefully.

Nature. So many gifts are available, but you've got to get out of your house and out of your car to appreciate them:

- Take a walk outside as often as possible. Not for exercise because to many, that is a chore. This walk is simply for the wonderful sights, scents and sounds you will encounter along the way. You may have driven down the road a million times in your car, but what you will discover on foot is an entirely different experience. For me, what I notice most are trees, flowers, butterflies, birds (and an occasional bunny!) I love how it all changes depending upon the location and the season. I have also recently discovered that if I get outside early in the morning, it's a whole different experience and a refreshing way to start the day. Even 5 minutes will do!
- Take photos of things you encounter and look back at them often. It'll transport you right back to that happy place.
- Get a hummingbird feeder (the best food recipe is available online – don't use the red stuff!) and observe these amazing creatures in action.
- Have a full-on conversation with your dog or cat. Be sure, however, that you don't burden them with complaints and frustrations. Tell them your dreams of the future or tell them

how much love they bring into your life. The conversation may make you laugh, and that makes it even more productive!
- Listen to the birds chirping for a few minutes, especially at sunrise or sunset when they are most vocal.
- Find a beautiful place to watch the sunset. Don't be afraid to go alone, but if that's not comfortable for you, take a pet, a child or someone who won't ruin the vibe with crankiness or negativity.
- Get up early enough so that you have a few moments alone in your home to enjoy your favorite music, reading material, the view, or just quiet time to think good thoughts. It's a great way to start your day!

Music (etc). Create a few playlists for specific purposes:

- Dance-able. What's that saying? "Dance like no one is watching"? So, do it! And if you crack yourself up, all the better!
- Calming. For use when meditating, or even as background music when you are working on a project. This will help with clarity, creativity, and absorption of information.
- Platforms such as YouTube for music with visuals such as ocean waves, rainforests and various nature settings.

Videos. This can be a fun trip down memory lane, or a hysterical adventure. It's about whatever makes you smile, sing, laugh or love.

- Funny animal videos.
- Comedians.
- Your favorite musicians (including the ones you rocked out to in your younger days!).
- Watch bloopers and gag reels from your favorite movies and TV shows.
- Re-watch movies or favorite scenes that you already know you love. That's the beauty of movies. Every time you watch your favorite feel-good movies, you get to feel good all over again!
- DIY projects that are of interest to you. You don't have to actually do them, just watch them and file the idea away for future reference.

Other:

- Watch a documentary about something positive or at least neutral. Give yourself a break from crime, scandal, disaster, politics, etc.
- Occasionally turn off media playing in your car and notice the environment around you. If you are driving in a peaceful location, open a window to take in the sounds and scents. If you find a location that makes you happy, go back there often.
- Do a puzzle. I suggest starting with a simple version so it's quick, easy and do-able…as opposed to a "project" that you may not have time for, and which could end up being a source of frustration rather than a happy distraction.
- Add come color to your world with adult coloring books. Use colorful pens and pencils. Or go outside and create with sidewalk chalk.
- Write. Make lists of things that make you happy, make you laugh, or sound like a lot of fun. Jot down your dreams. It doesn't have to be an official journal, just a notepad or even scraps of paper. Anything that will allow you to regularly revisit your joy.
- Collect photos. Cut them out or screenshot them and save to a file or album. I am not necessarily referring to a "vision board." I mean things that make you feel good when you observe them. For example, places, animals, fashion, landscape, architecture, etc.
- The Gratitude Jar. Every time something good happens to you, write it down and place the piece of paper in an empty jar. At the end of the week, month, or year, empty the jar and see how many gifts life has given you. Be grateful.

Appreciate. There is so much to appreciate, and it takes no time at all. Look for things throughout your day to appreciate:

- The weather
- Your family
- Blue skies
- People who make you laugh
- Your body; that amazing vehicle that gets you through life
- People who love you
- Best friends
- Your pets
- Children's laughter

- Your snuggly bed, sheets and pillow
- Hugs and kisses
- Compliments
- Freedom
- Nature
- Sunrises and sunsets
- Love

Daydream. Often. This is so much fun, but it only works if you dream really big! If you dream about things that are currently in your experience, reality gets in the way and doubt will kill the fun. So for purposes of this exercise, limit your thoughts to things and people who are not currently part of your life.

Make friends with your mirror. Every time you encounter a mirror, look at your reflection, stare deeply into your eyes, and say out loud, "Hi, Friend."

This book:

Just remember that fun, easy, happy things are typically not served up to you from external sources as often as the negative and stressful things are. So you've got to practice Happy.

This book is intended to be an easy go-to distraction for you. So keep it handy, and whenever you need a quick fix, head for Chapter 12- **The Inspiration.**

- Read through several entries to give yourself a bit of laughter or joy anytime.
- Read an entry, or a few, or several, right before going to bed so the last thing on your mind before you drift off to sleep is something fun or inspirational.
- Read an entry, or a few, or several before you get out of bed in the morning. Start your day on a positive and happy note.
- If the book is helpful for you, share it with a friend who may benefit from it. It's a gift of Happy that will keep giving.

12. THE INSPIRATION

Oh, my God…

What if you wake up some day and you're 65 or 75 and you never got your memoir written; or you didn't go swimming in warm pools and oceans all those years because your thighs were jiggly and you had a nice big comfortable tummy; and you were just so strung out on perfectionism and people-pleasing that you forgot to have a big juicy creative life of imagination and radical silliness and staring off into space like when you were a kid? It's going to break your heart. Don't let this happen.

~ Anne Lamott

The door to happiness...

opens from the inside.

Darling girl

Let today

be about the things

that make you happy.

Maybe life

isn't about avoiding the bruises.

Maybe it's about collecting the scars

to prove we showed up for it.

I'm learning

to love the sound of my feet

walking away from things

not meant for me.

He asked

"Are you free tomorrow?"

I replied

"No, I'm expensive every day."

Sometimes

I shock myself with the smart stuff

I say and do.

Other times,

I try to get out of the car

with my seat belt on.

You are

no longer a part of my life,

but I wish you

the best with yours.

~ Mario Tomasello

My goal

is to build a life

I don't need a vacation from.

~ Rob Hill, Sr

Burn the candles.

Use the nice sheets.

Wear the fancy lingerie.

Don't save it

for a special occasion.

Today is special.

~ Regina Brett

Behind every strong woman

is a dog that follows her

to the bathroom.

Giving up on a goal

because of a setback

is like slashing

your other 3 tires

because you got a flat.

Be with someone

who ruins your lipstick,

not your mascara.

Don't look back.

You aren't going that way.

To remember

who *you* are,

you need to forget

who they told you to be.

You are only given
a little spark of madness.
You mustn't lose it.

~ Robin Williams

Remember when

plastic surgery was a taboo subject?

Now you mention Botox

and nobody raises an eyebrow.

My wrinkles

are all from laughter.

Well, except those lines

between my eyebrows.

Those are my "WTF?" lines,

and those things are deep.

Sometimes

life is about risking everything

for a dream

nobody else can see.

I can

and I will…

because I'm badass like that.

Life status:

Currently holding it together

with one bobby pin.

DIANE BUCCOLA

My dentist

told me I needed a crown.

I was like, "I know! Right?"

Trying

to make protein shakes,

but they keep coming out

as margaritas.

Ah, kindness.

What a simple way

to tell another struggling soul

that there is *love* to be found

in this world.

~ A.A. Malee

My brain:

"I see you are trying to sleep. May I offer you a selection of your worst memories from the last 10 years?"

Honestly,

I don't have time

to hate people who hate me,

because I'm too busy loving

the people who love me.

Don't be sad

because it's over.

Be glad because it happened.

~ Dr. Seuss

DIANE BUCCOLA

I love

the woman I am

because I fought to become her.

~ Ilovemylsi

For beautiful eyes,

look for the good in others.

For beautiful lips,

speak only words of kindness.

And for poise,

walk with the knowledge

that you are never alone.

~ Audrey Hepburn

When life

knocks you down,

just stay there and take a nap.

~ Rumi

The greater the storm,

the brighter the rainbow.

Cinderella

never asked for a Prince.

She asked for a night off

and a dress.

~ Kiera Cass

The trouble with women

is that they get all excited

about nothing…

and then they marry him.

~ Cher

Darling,

I never step on a scale

because the scale

doesn't measure sexy.

~ Bella Doce

Admire

someone else's beauty

without questioning your own.

DIANE BUCCOLA

Don't judge me

until you've flown a mile

on my broom.

One Life.

Just one.

Why aren't we running

like we are on fire

towards our wildest dreams?

I will not

compare myself

to a stranger on Instagram.

You are

part of a puzzle

in someone's life.

You may never know

where you fit.

But someone's life

may never be complete

without you in it.

~ Malika E Nura

Sometimes

I question my sanity.

But the unicorn in the kitchen

told me I'm fine.

Remember that girl

who gave up?

Neither does anyone else.

When you hold grudges,

your hands aren't free

to catch blessings.

Sometimes

you will not realize

the true value of a moment...

until it becomes

a memory.

You don't like me?

That's a shame.

I'll need a few minutes to recover

from this tragedy.

Joy is contagious...

we catch it from our friends.

You don't

have to be crazy

to be my friend.

I'll train you.

The best thing I ever did

was believe in myself.

I just hugged you

in my thoughts.

I hope you felt it.

It always seems impossible... until it's done.

~ Nelson Mandela

I stopped giving advice.

Now I give compliments.

We're all happier.

Years from now,

I won't remember

every Friday night

or the things

that made me laugh so hard

'til my stomach hurt.

But I will always remember

who was there with me.

It's okay

to let go of friends

who no longer fit.

In case

no one told you today,

I'm beautiful.

I love

the smell of freshly brewed coffee

in the morning.

And I love

the sound of no one talking to me

while I drink it.

Don't regret

growing older.

It's a privilege denied to many.

~ Ritu Ghadouery

When she transformed

into a butterfly,

the caterpillars spoke;

not of her beauty,

but of her weirdness.

They wanted her

to change back

into what she had always been.

But she had wings.

~ Dean Jackson

"Once upon a time"

...is really *here and now.*

~ Angi Sullins

Being negative

only makes a difficult journey

more difficult.

You may be given a cactus,

but you don't have to sit on it.

People who inspire others

are those who see

invisible bridges

at the end of dead-end streets.

~ Charles Swindoll

When you're in a dark place,

you sometimes tend to think

you've been buried.

Perhaps you've been planted.

Bloom.

You'll know

the people who feed your soul,

because you'll feel good

after spending time with them.

Little by little,

day by day,

what's meant for you

will find its way.

My darling girl,

When are you going to realize

that being "normal"

is not necessarily a virtue?

It sometimes denotes

a lack of courage.

~ Alice Hoffman

A woman has two problems:

Nothing to wear.

No room for all her clothes.

I live in my own world,

but it's okay...

they know me here.

I think

aging is an extraordinary process

whereby you become

the person

you always should have been.

~ David Bowie

You know, dear...

karma's only a bitch

if you are.

If you're still

looking for that one person

who will change your life...

take a look in the mirror.

~ Roman Prince

You need

to hang out with people

who fit your future,

not your history.

Whatever

you talk about,

or even think about,

becomes part of your experience.

Choose carefully.

Throughout the day,

I count my blessings

one-by-one.

Whatever, or whomever,

you believe is controlling

your life,

is controlling your life.

Don't give away your power.

I can be social.

Today I meowed at my cat,

and he meowed back.

Happiness

is not a destination.

It is a way of life.

When something goes wrong in your life, just yell "PLOT TWIST!" and move on.

Whatever

makes my soul feel good,

that's what I'm going to chase.

I can't wait

To walk down the aisle again someday

and hear those magical words:

"This is your pilot speaking."

A good life

is when you smile often,

dream big,

laugh a lot,

and realize how blessed you are

for what you have.

NOTES FROM YOUR FAIRY GODMOTHER

I hope

you live a life you are proud of;

if you find you are not,

I hope you find the strength

to start over all over again.

F. Scott Fitzgerald

Two words

for those who don't think

shoes are important:

Cinderella and Dorothy.

A real woman

avoids drama.

She knows her time is precious

and she's not wasting it

on unimportant things.

Can't see all the haters

when I've got my

love glasses on.

Difficult roads

often lead to beautiful

destinations.

~ Melchor Lim

She was beautiful,

but not like those girls

in the magazines.

She was beautiful

for the way she thought.

She was beautiful

for the sparkle in her eyes

when she talked about

something she loved.

She was beautiful

for her ability

to make other people smile,

even if she was sad.

If you love someone,

set them free.

If they come back,

it means nobody else liked them.

Set them free again.

Life is short,

eat the cookies

(and buy the shoes).

Good friends

help you to find

important things

when you have lost them.

Your smile,

your hope

and your courage.

~ Doe Zantamata

A woman

is unstoppable

after she realizes

she deserves better.

Thank you, my love.

I am going to keep

all the beautiful memories

and lovely moments

you've gifted me...

and accept the many lessons

that came my way.

And most importantly,

I am letting go of any negativity

that could possibly diminish

my future joy.

I have learned

that caring for myself

is not being self-indulgent.

It is self-preservation

and is vital to my health.

What made her strong

was that despite

the millions of things that hurt her,

she spoke of nothing

but happiness.

When I try on an outfit

and it doesn't make me look good,

I just throw it on the floor

like, *"No!*

You don't deserve to be hung up.

Sit there and think about

what you've done."

What if I fall?

Oh, but my darling,

what if you fly?

~ Erin Hanson

Beauty

isn't about having a pretty face.

It's about having a pretty heart,

a pretty mind,

and a pretty soul.

~ Drake

Here's to strong women.

May we know them.

May we be them.

May we raise them.

I'm just a girl

standing in front of a Tuesday

asking it to be a Friday.

I never make the same mistake twice. I make it five or six times, just to be sure.

They say

with age comes wisdom.

Therefore, I don't have wrinkles.

I have *wise* cracks.

Find a partner

who strokes your hair

and says how soft it is,

and doesn't even care

that it's on your legs.

Don't let anyone

ruin your day.

It's your day…

ruin it yourself,

A woman

unaffected by insults

has made her enemies

powerless.

And suddenly

you know...

It's time to start something new

and trust the magic of

beginnings.

~ Meister Eckhart

I don't think

inside the box.

I don't think

outside the box either.

I don't even know

where the box is!

I do not need

your approval, darling.

That's for insecure people.

Behind every successful woman... is a best friend giving her crazy ideas.

People often wonder

if the glass is half empty

or half full…

but they're missing the point.

The glass is refillable.

Dance

like no one is watching.

But text, post and email

like it will be read in court someday.

I know my limits.

I don't pay attention to them…

but I know them.

When you talk,

You are only repeating

what you already know.

But if you listen,

you may learn something new.

~ Dalai Lama

The older I get,

the more I understand

that it's okay to live a life

that others don't understand.

Your journey

will be much lighter and easier

if you don't carry your past with you.

Dearly Beloved.

We are gathered here today

to get through this thing

called life.

~ Prince

Bad News:

You're not going to fit in.

Good News:

The great ones never do.

I'm pretty sure

My dream job would be

a Karma delivery person.

Your mission:

To be so busy loving your life that you have no time for hate, regret or fear.

~ *Karen Salmansohn*

Mirror, mirror,

on the wall.

It does not matter

if I'm short or tall...

If I have skinny legs

or my hips are wide...

It only matters who I am inside.

Blue eyes, brown eyes,

black or green...

What makes me beautiful

cannot be seen.

When you look at me,

don't judge my parts.

The most beautiful thing about me

is my heart.

The bad news:

There is no key to happiness.

The good news: It isn't locked.

With a little rain,

she found her rainbow.

I believe in pink.

I believe that laughing

is the best calorie burner.

I believe in kissing…kissing a lot.

I believe in being strong

when everything seems

to be going wrong.

I believe that happy girls

are the prettiest girls.

I believe that tomorrow

is another day,

and I believe in miracles.

~ Audrey Hepburn

Waking up

is never easy.

But I just have to remind myself

that the world can't revolve around me

unless I get out of bed.

When life

gives you rainy days,

wear cute boots

and jump in the puddles.

Let us be grateful

to people who make us happy.

They are the charming

gardeners who make

our souls blossom.

~ Marcel Proust

Don't let

people discourage you.
Just fluff out your tutu
and twirl away.

I'd walk through fire

for my best friend.

Well, maybe not fire…

that would be dangerous.

But a super humid room…

but not too humid,

because, you know, my hair.

The only things you can take with you when you leave this world are things you have packed inside your heart.

~ Susan Gale

The grass is greener

where you water it.

~ Neil Barringham

You survived

what you thought

would kill you.

Now straighten your crown

and move forward

like the Queen that you are.

Wrinkles

mean you laughed,

grey hair means you cared,

and scars mean you lived.

I had a date last night

and I really enjoyed it.

So tonight,

I'm going to try a fig.

It doesn't matter

who you love,

or how you love,

but that you love.

~ Rod McKuen

Before

going to sleep at night,

forgive everyone

and sleep with a clean heart.

(Not for them...for you.)

If I cannot

do great things,

I can do small things

in a great way.

~ *Martin Luther King, Jr.*

Mother said

I could be anything I want.

I decided to be confident.

It's okay

if you fall down

and lose your spark.

Just make sure

that when you get back up,

you rise as the whole damn fire.

~ Colette Werden

If you feel

like you don't fit in this world,

it is because

you are here to help create a new one.

A successful woman

takes the bricks the devil

throws at her and uses them

to lay a firm foundation.

~ Nishan Panwar

Women are angels.

And when someone breaks our wings,

we simply continue to fly

on a broomstick.

We're flexible like that.

DIANE BUCCOLA

I missed myself.

I'm glad she's coming back.

Some people

create their own storms

and then get mad when it rains.

At the end of the day,

I am thankful that my blessings are bigger than my problems.

When you see

something beautiful

in someone, tell them.

It may take only seconds to say

but for them,

it could last a lifetime.

Sometimes

the grass is greener on the

other side...

because it's fake.

When life shuts a door...

open it again.

It's a door.

That's how they work.

Sometimes

you find yourself

in the middle of nowhere.

And sometimes

in the middle of nowhere,

you find yourself.

Life is a buffet of choices. There is no need to condemn the options you didn't choose.

Some days,

I wish I could go back in life.

Not to change anything,

but to feel a few things twice.

Life's as kind

as the people you fill it with.

One day,

she remembered

that it wasn't her job

to make everyone happy.

I want

every little girl

whose has been told she's bossy

to instead be told

she has leadership skills.

What if

you devoted this entire year

to loving yourself more?

When you meet the one

who changes the way

your heart beats,

dance with them to that rhythm

for as long as the song lasts.

~ Kirk Diedrich

Hula Blessing:

May you have

Grace in your step,

Song in your hand,

and Aloha in your heart.

I don't regret

burning my bridges.

I do regret

that certain people

weren't on those bridges.

Often

in the winds of change,

a new direction is found.

Logic will take you

from point A to point B.

Imagination will take you everywhere.

~ Albert Einstein

DIANE BUCCOLA

Forgiveness

has nothing to do

with an apology.

Would you rather

be right..or happy?

(Be selfish, choose happy!)

Sometimes

you need to look back.

Just to find

where you dropped your standards,

lost your confidence,

and started settling

for less than you deserve.

Once you discover that place,

pick them back up,

make peace

with that time in your life,

and march on

with your head held high.

A good friend knows all your stories. A best friend helped you write them.

I am going to make everything around me more beautiful. That will be my life.

~ Elise de Wolfe

If it makes you giggle,

then do it again

(and again and again...)

DIANE BUCCOLA

I am learning

to love the sound of my feet

walking away from things

not meant for me.

If I had

a single Flower

for every time

I think about you,

I could walk in my Garden forever.

~ Chanda Ghandi

When you are

comfortable on your path,

it doesn't matter where it leads.

~ Abraham Hicks

Stay afraid,

but do it anyway.

What's important is the action.

You don't have to wait

to be confident.

Just do it...and eventually

the confidence will follow.

~ *Carrie Fisher*

Although

great lessons are learned

from a glance in

the rear-view mirror,

if you keep looking backward,

you're going to crash.

When we argue for our limitations… we get to keep them.

~ *Evelyn Waugh*

Don't let

your struggle

become your identity.

~ Ralston Bowles

NOTES FROM YOUR FAIRY GODMOTHER

Embrace

the glorious mess that you are.

~Elizabeth Gilbert

Behind every

girl's favorite song,

there's an untold story.

Imagination

is the only weapon

in the war against reality.

~ Lewis Carroll

Stars can't shine

without darkness.

~ D.H. Sidebottom

Just because my path is different doesn't mean I'm lost.

~ Gerard Abrams

You don't have to

see the whole staircase.

Just take the first step.

~ Martin Luther King, Jr.

These mountains

that you are carrying...

you were only

supposed to climb.

~ Najwa Zebian

Know that

you can start late,

look different, be uncertain,

and still succeed.

~ Misty Copeland

You want

to come into my life,

the door is open.

You want to get out of my life,

the door is open.

Just one request:

Don't stand at the door,

you're blocking traffic.

If you

learned something,

then it wasn't a waste of time.

Sometimes

the best way to determine

what you *do* want

is to first clarify

what you *don't* want.

~ Abraham Hicks

My friends

have made the story of my life.

~ Helen Keller

Sometimes
the right thing feels all wrong
until it is over and done with.

~ Alice Hoffman

It takes courage

to remove yourself from people,

places and things

that don't bring you joy.

Be brave, dear one,

and see where your joy leads you.

For every minute

you are angry,

you lose sixty seconds

of happiness.

~ Ralph Waldo Emerson

There is no path

to happiness.

Happiness *is* the path.

My world

is brighter and more beautiful

because of you.

Thank you.

~ Malika E Nura

Detox your life

by clearing out fake friends,

dead-end jobs,

and players posing as partners.

~ Ritu Ghatourey

We can't always

choose the music life plays for us.

But we can choose how we dance to it.

And then

my soul saw you

and kind of went

"Oh, there you are.

I've been looking for you."

I'm erasing

all the unwanted drama

out of my life…

because at the end of the day,

I'm just trying to be happy.

~ Mario Tomasello

Beautiful girl.

You can do hard things.

When your ex
asks if you can still be friends
right after a breakup,
it's like having a kidnapper
telling you to keep in touch.

DIANE BUCCOLA

I hope

you will have a wonderful year,

that you'll dream

dangerously and outrageously,

that you'll make something

that didn't exist before you made it,

that you will be loved

and that you will be liked,

and that you will have people to love

and to like in return.

And, most importantly

(because I think there should be

more kindness and more wisdom

in the world right now),

that you will, when you need to be,

be wise, and that you will always

be kind.

~ Neil Gaiman

We are so much more powerful and important than we realize. In each moment that we connect with another, we have the opportunity to etch a memory into their heart.

~ Robin Lee

And yet again

this morning,

no one was standing next to my bed

saying, "Your Royal Highness,

here is your coffee."

If we magnified our successes as much as we magnify our disappointments, we'd all be much happier.

~ Abraham Lincoln

DIANE BUCCOLA

Lessons

come in layers,

like an onion.

Get your facts first,

then you can distort them

as you please.

~ Mark Twain

Don't allow

your wounds

to transform you

into someone you're not.

~ Paulo Coelho

I'm happy.

Which often looks like crazy.

~ David Henry Hwang

DIANE BUCCOLA

Never

let anyone

dull your sparkle.

Love is

Falling asleep on the sofa

and waking up

with a blanket on you.

Underneath the chaos

of everyday life

is a sacred space within.

Where dreams are conceived,

wisdom breathes

and love is experienced

from the inside out.

It is serenity, peace,

and the bliss of simply being.

Your circle

should want you to win.

Your circle should clap the loudest

when you have good news.

If they don't, get a new circle.

And now...

I'll do what's best for me.

Your Fairy Godmother lives within *you*...

So, Darling Girl,

let today be about the things

that make you happy.

ABOUT THE AUTHOR

Diane Buccola is an NCEA Certified Esthetician, licensed in the state of California since 1999. She is a Spa Consultant, Author, and Speaker for the spa industry. Diane is the author of "The Heart of Esthetics: Creating Loyal Clients and Achieving Financial Success" and "Estheticians are a Girl's Best Friend."

www.ingramcontent.com/pod-product-compliance
Lightning Source LLC
Chambersburg PA
CBHW050532300426
44113CB00012B/2064

One Life. Just *one*.
Why then aren't we running at full speed toward the life of our dreams?

Ever wonder why some people seem to be happy in spite of life's ups and downs, and everything always seems to go well for them? Is it because they have lived an obstacle-free life? Or do they have a superpower that you don't know about? Of course not. In fact, what they have is available to us all. Some learn it early in life, some never learn it at all, and the rest of us learn it eventually. So let your "eventually" begin right now!

Notes from Your Fairy Godmother offers ideas, inspiration, and motivation to help you shift your focus, rediscover your joy, and live the happy life you can and should be living, regardless of what may be happening in your life or the world around you. Also included are over 200 quotes, reflections, and happy thoughts to motivate and inspire you and keep you steadily on the path to your dreams.

"Once upon a Time" is here and now. So, Darling Girl, let today be about the things that make you happy.

DIANE BUCCOLA is an NCEA Certified Esthetician, spa consultant, author, and speaker at international trade shows for the spa industry. She is the author of "The Heart of Esthetics: Creating Loyal Clients & Achieving Financial Success" and "Estheticians are a Girl's Best Friend."

ISBN 978-0-9986709-0-4

The NEW CRYSTAL CODES

Align Your Crystals To The New Energies

CRYSTAL CODES, CIPHERS AND FUNCTIONS
FOR THE NEW ERA
New: ALIGN YOUR CRYSTALS
CHOOSING AND WORKING WITH CRYSTALS

Learn the difference between an Isis, a Record-Keeper, a Lemurian and many more...

Sets of crystals to assist in love, success, protection, life stress

MYRA SRI